Scenes
From
The Life

A Collection Of Monologues, Sketches, And A Short Play

Joseph McBee

CSS Publishing Company, Inc., Lima, Ohio

SCENES FROM THE LIFE

Copyright © 2005 by
CSS Publishing Company, Inc.
Lima, Ohio

For more information about CSS Publishing Company resources, visit our website at www.csspub.com or e-mail us at custserv@csspub.com or call (800) 241-4056.

Cover design by Chris Patton
ISBN 0-7880-2358-6   PRINTED IN U.S.A.

For the Arts Ministry
of City Harvest Worship Center

Table Of Contents

Introduction

The power of story cannot be overstated. The prophets of old used story to express the heart of God. Our Lord Jesus himself used story to express the truths of the kingdom. The early church fathers used story to express the realities of the cross and a life lived in service to God.

Somewhere along the way, the church lost sight of the power of story to help us define and understand the truth of our existence, both with and without Christ.

Recently, however, we have begun to see a resurgence of the use of theater, film, and story in the church. This is a good thing. It gives handles to the preaching of the word. It is something for people to hold onto as they grapple with the truth, trying to understand it and assimilate it into their lives. It helps to tear down walls of resistance and make the truth easier to receive.

Sometimes the truth makes us laugh, sometimes cry, and sometimes even wince from the sharpness of it. The offerings in this collection were created to do that very thing.

For I believe that above everything else, artists, particularly Christian artists, exist to tell the truth: creatively, with beauty, power, and style, but always to tell the truth.

The sketches and monologues in this book can be used as sermon illustrators or entertainment pieces. They examine various aspects of the Christian life in a humorous and poignant style covering everything from faith to gossip, and conviction to nursery work.

The pieces in this book have minimal sets and props and small casts in order to make them accessible to church drama groups of all sizes.

Many of the pieces in this book, if grouped together, can be used as an entire evening of entertainment, as well.

All Quiet On The Front Pew

Cast

Vernon Hunt: *A church member*
Velma Hunt: *Vernon's wife*
August Potter: *Another church member*
Helen Potter: *August's wife*
Bill Hicks: *An usher*
Usher: *You guessed it, an usher*
Pastor Lewis: *The senior pastor*

Props

Two WWII-style army helmets, an offering plate or basket, two blindfolds, two Bibles, a pew or four chairs, and two pairs of earmuffs.

Costumes

The characters are in your church, so they should dress like the members of your church ordinarily do.

———————

(When the lights come up, Vernon, Velma, August, and Helen are all seated center stage on a pew facing the audience. They are preparing for the service to start. Vernon and August look very nervous. They keep looking over their shoulders as if they expect to be attacked from behind.)

Velma: Vernon Hunt will you please stop looking over your shoulder like a nervous little chihuahua? We are in church.

Vernon: I know we're in church, Velma, why do you think I'm so nervous?

Velma: What are you talking about?

Vernon: Tell her, August.

August: Things got a little uncomfortable the last time we were here.

Helen: How?

August: You wouldn't understand Helen. You're a woman.

Helen: What is that supposed to mean?

Vernon: It means that women are just naturally more spiritual than men, so they can be a little more comfortable in church.

Velma: That's ridiculous. I've never heard such nonsense. Pastor Lewis is a man and he's so spiritual he *works* in a church.

August: Pastors don't count, they are a different breed.

Helen: What about Bill Hicks? He serves as an usher every Sunday.

Vernon and August: Brainwashed.

Velma: Are you two crazy?

Vernon: Call us what you will, but have you ever seen the look in his eyes?

August: And that smile on his face *every* Sunday?

Vernon: It's just not normal.

August: It's not right. Remember old Frank Carter?

Helen: What about him?

Vernon: He was another victim.

August: Pastor Lewis preached a sermon on servanthood and Frank got all fired up, said he wanted to *do something for God.*

Vernon: A week later, he became the Sunday School Director.

August: Another casualty of war.

Helen: Casualty of war?

August: That's right. We're at war, and the price could be our very comfort and convenience. Why, if some stray bullet of conviction were to strike us, there's no telling what would happen.

Vernon: We might volunteer to help in the children's church or something.

August: Or start reading our Bibles.

Vernon: Or heaven forbid ...

August and Vernon: Tithe! *(both shudder at the horror of the thought)*

Velma: For goodness sake, you two are a sorry sight. Now get hold of yourselves, the song service is starting.

Vernon: Ready, August?

August: Ready, Vernon.

(August and Vernon pick up their earmuffs and put them on. Velma and Helen stand and begin to move their mouths as if singing. August and Vernon sit with their arms crossed in front of them. Periodically they look at each other and grin or give a thumbs-up sign. After a few moments of this Velma and Helen sit down and Vernon and August remove their earmuffs.)

11

Velma: Well you certainly avoided any conviction there.

Vernon: That was easy, we haven't gotten into the thick of the battle yet.

Pastor Lewis: *(offstage)* Now we have come to the part of our service where we will receive the Lord's tithes and our offerings.

(Bill and Usher enter from behind. Bill is carrying an offering plate. He comes to stand beside Vernon. Usher takes a position beside August at the other end of the row.)

Bill: Vernon, how are you this morning?

Vernon: Pretty good up until now, Bill. *(pauses)* Now, August!

(Vernon and August lift up blindfolds and put them on)

Bill: Mind if I ask what you're doing?

Vernon: If we don't see the plate, we don't have to give.

Bill: That's a strange kind of theology, don't you think?

Vernon: I'd appreciate it if you wouldn't use that kind of language around me, Bill.

Velma: *(taking the offering plate)* Ignore him Bill, he's been under a lot of stress lately. I'm considering getting him some professional help.

Bill: Good idea. *(the plate gets passed to the end of the row to Usher, Usher and Bill exit)*

Velma: The coast is clear, soldier. You can come out now.

Vernon: Mock me if you will, but I'm not taking any chances.

Pastor Lewis: *(offstage)* And now if you will open your Bibles, we will begin today's sermon....

August: Incoming!

(Vernon and August dive behind the pew and put on army helmets. They put on their earmuffs and duck behind the pew as if they are dodging bullets. Velma and Helen are horribly embarrassed but compose themselves well enough to listen to the sermon. After a few moments, the sermon ends. August and Vernon remove their earmuffs and helmets and come out from behind the pew. They shake hands and begin to congratulate each other on their success.)

Vernon: Another successful campaign.

August: There were a few close calls.

Vernon: Yeah, I almost saw that offering plate.

August: Don't think about that now.

Vernon: Let's just put it behind us.

Pastor Lewis: *(enters stage right and crosses to Vernon)* Vernon Hunt, just the man I wanted to see! I would really appreciate it if you would be an usher this quarter. Bill Hicks has just been telling me that you have some very interesting ideas about tithing and he thinks you're an ideal candidate for that ministry. What do you say?

(Vernon staggers back as if he has been shot. Pastor Lewis exits stage right. Vernon falls to the ground, and August rushes to his side.)

August: We've got a wounded man here. Medic!

Blackout

13

The Great Church Trade-in

Cast
   Honest Bill Kline: *A new and used church salesman*

Props
   None

Costumes
   An incredibly loud and obnoxious suit (much like the character himself)

———————————————

(Honest Bill Kline is standing center stage as the lights come up. As soon as lights are up, he should launch into his commercial.)

Honest Bill Kline: Hi, folks. Honest Bill Kline here at Kline's Churches, Denominations, and Ministries and have I got a deal for you!

This week, that's right, this week only, we are hosting the world's largest church trade-in. That's right folks, this week only you can bring in that old church of yours and trade it in for one of our top of the line models. All of our churches are priced to go, and we'll take anything in trade, that's right, *anything!*

Have a collision with your pastor because he didn't shake your hand on Sunday morning and you just don't think you can *receive* from his ministry any more? Don't try and work it out, don't try and adjust your attitude, just *come on down* because I've got a deal for you. You can get into a new church where the pastor is afraid of your attitude. That way you can gripe, complain, and be petty all you want and he'll never say a word, because after all, he wants to make sure he keeps his job.

Is your church too old and boring for you? Do they sing too many hymns and is the teaching just a little too *theological?* Well, *come on down* because I've got a deal for you! I'll get you into a young, fresh, and exciting church with little to no depth at all!

Granted it is a little too sporty to accommodate anyone with wisdom and maturity, but who needs wisdom when you've got zeal?

Does your church require too much out of you? Do you feel like you always have to be committed when you'd rather just sit and warm a pew? Well, *come on down*, because I've got a deal for you! You can have a new church that is designed to meet all of your needs without requiring you to do a thing! That's right, no commitment required. We will even take one, two, three, even four percent off of your tithe, that's right you can get a six percent tithe at one of these babies. This type of church doesn't last long, so hurry on down to Honest Bill Kline's Churches, Denominations, and Ministries because I've got a deal for you.

Blackout

Honk If You Love Jesus

Cast
Harry: *A Christian who is giving a friend a ride home*
Bob: *Harry's friend*

Prop
Two chairs

Costumes
Both men should look like they are on their way home from work.

Production Notes
This sketch can also be done with two women. (Of course you will want to change the names)

(Harry and Bob are sitting on two chairs at center stage. Harry is driving with a smile on his face. Bob is looking out the window.)

Harry: Beautiful evening isn't it, Bob?

Bob: Sure is. I hope I can catch a little daylight when I get home so I can mow my lawn. But with all this traffic, I don't know if I'm gonna make it.

Harry: You know rush hour. Although I must admit that I'm glad the traffic is so bad today. There is something I want to talk to you about.

Bob: Okay, shoot.

Harry: *(screams and turns sharply to the left and then straightens the car out again, and yells at the offending driver)* Hey, you moron! Look where you're going! Did you get your license out of

17

your cereal box this morning or what? *(to Bob)* Can you believe that guy? Jerks like that really put me in a bad mood.

Bob: *(pauses, startled by Harry's reaction)* Yeah ... I know what you mean. *(beat)* What was it that you wanted to talk to me about?

Harry: *(remembering)* Oh, yeah. I actually wanted to talk to you about your relationship with God.

Bob: Yeah, I was afraid of that. Look, I know where you're headed and ...

Harry: *(to another driver)* Hey, you jerk, where do you think you're going? *(stomps on the gas)* You're not getting in front of me, lady! *(passes the other driver and then slows, then to Bob)* What was it you were saying?

Bob: *(pauses)* I was saying that I know where you're going with this and I'm really not interested. I know *you're* a Christian, and that's fine, but it's just not for me.

Harry: Not for you? Not interested? Bob I'm talking about your relationship with God here, I'm not trying to sell you a timeshare or something. You've got to be interested in your relationship with God.

Bob: Not really. No offense, Harry, but I don't see that big of a difference between people who say they know God and myself. I'm doing just fine on my own.

Harry: I know where you're coming from, and I used to think the same thing myself. But then I realized that I was a *mess* without Christ. Once I became a Christian, I was changed. I'm different now. I live by a higher standard. *(looks at driver in front of him)* Oh, come on! Get going, pal, the rest of us have a life to get on with here!

Bob: Harry, he's got to be going eighty miles an hour.

Harry: I know! Can you believe he has the nerve to drive in the fast lane? *(beat)* Like I was saying before, I'm a different man. That only happens in a relationship with God through Jesus. In fact Jesus said, no one comes to the Father except through ... my exit, you jerk!

Bob: Did Jesus really say that?

Harry: *(to another driver)* I said that's my exit, you jerk, now move it!

Bob: Oh. *(brief pause)* Look, Harry, I like my life. I like the fact that I can choose my own beliefs, my own path. I don't want to live by a big list of do's and don'ts.

Harry: It's not about rules. It's about being free. Christianity is about being ... a kid who is going too slow on his bike down the middle of the road! *(leans out of his window)* Hey, kid! Why don't you ride your bike on the expressway and get out of my way. *(looks at Bob and laughs but notices that Bob is furious)*

Bob: That's my son, Harry.

Harry: Oops. Sorry. *(pauses)* You have to admit that he is a little slow on that bike.

Bob: Why don't you stop the car and let me out here. I'd like to walk with my son the rest of the way home. *(Harry brings the car to a stop and Bob gets out and exits)*

Harry: *(yells after him)* I never said Christians were perfect ... just forgiven! *(pauses, sighs, and shrugs his shoulders)* Oh well, Harry, don't get discouraged, just keep living the life and he'll come around.

Blackout

19

The Prayer Request

Cast
Woman: *A busybody who is very "concerned" about her friends*

Props
None

Costumes
Modern

(Woman enters stage left. When she reaches center stage she looks out into the audience as if she is recognizing a particular person. The entire monologue will be delivered to that "person.")

Woman: Well, good morning, sister! How are you this fine and glorious morning? Isn't it wonderful to be in the house of the Lord? *(pauses and thinks for a moment, then looks around to make sure no one else is listening before she speaks)*

Sister, I really sense in my spirit that I need to share a prayer request with you concerning Jed and Elma. I am telling you this in the strictest confidence, so just keep it to yourself so you can pray about it.

Jed and Elma are having some serious trouble with their son Ronny. And I mean *big* trouble ... I know, I always thought he was a good boy, too, but I have certainly changed my opinion after what I've heard.

(pauses) Oh I don't know if I should divulge the details ... well, if you need to know so your prayers can be more specific then I guess it would be all right. But remember, this goes no further that the two of us darlin'.

(looks around again) According to what Johnny told me, Ronny was out with some of his friends the other night and they were pulled over by the police because they were driving too fast and

they were all arrested for being drunk. And Ronny's only seventeen years old! Why, who knows what he'll be into next? I'll bet you anything he's smoking pot and skipping school. Next thing you know he'll be involved in some gang, and they'll find him out on the streets dealing smack and carrying a gun. Then he'll be the subject of a multi-state manhunt after he shoots some poor soul and before you know it he'll be in the gas chamber with his parents suffering something awful. Don't you know they are so embarrassed? I wouldn't come out of my house if I had a drug-dealing, gun-toting, gang-banger for a son.

Now I know what you're thinking but believe you me, Johnny is a reliable source. He is a close personal friend of Betty Jo's and you know how close Betty Jo is to Thelma Lou who was told by Wilma who has been doing Nancy's hair for years, and Nancy is Elma's Sunday school teacher and best friend in the world, so it is practically from the horse's mouth, as they say.

Remember, honey, Johnny told me not to tell a soul because Betty Jo told her that Thelma Lou said that Wilma told her that Nancy said that Jed and Elma wanted it kept quiet. So you just keep it to yourself so you can pray about it. Okay, honey? *(pauses)* I knew I could count on you sister. You and I are a part of the more spiritual bunch around here. We just can't help but be burdened by the pain, misery, and suffering of others. We just have to let it out don't we? In prayer, that is.

How are you doing, honey? *(pauses)* Really? Why that is just terrible sweetie, I had no idea it was that bad ... No ... he didn't! *(pauses)* He did? Why, I never in all my life ... I just don't believe it. *(pauses)* Of course I won't breathe a word to anyone. You know I'm as silent as the grave, the very picture of discretion. *(notices someone offstage right)* Excuse me, honey, I see someone else I need to speak to. *(crosses stage and speaks as she does)* Michael! I got a prayer request for you, honey! *(exits)*

Blackout

22

The Nursery Zone

Cast
Narrator: *A Rod Serling type*
Joel: *A volunteer nursery worker*
Hank: *Another worker*
David: *Another worker*
Debbie: *Joel's wife*
Leah: *Hank's wife*
Mary: *David's wife*

Props
None

Costumes
Modern

(Sketch opens with Twilight Zone *music playing.)*

Narrator: *(offstage)* Travel with us now on a journey to a place where nothing is outside the realm of possibility, a place where anything *can* and usually *does* happen. Come with us to a place just outside the sanctuary. Look there's a sign post up ahead. We've just entered ... The Nursery Zone. *(enters stage right and crosses to center stage and begins to address the audience)*
    Enter three women *(Debbie, Leah, and Mary enter stage right)* the wives of three men who just finished their first tour of duty in the church nursery. A sermon on service from the pastor sent these men hurtling down the dark chasm of volunteer nursery work. Will they survive the experience? Or will they be forever changed by their time here? For people *are* changed in ... The Nursery Zone. *(exits)*

Mary: Wow, the service went a little long today.

Debbie: A little long? I counted five "in closings" and four "in conclusions."

Leah: Not to mention singing the sixteen verses of that closing song.

Mary: I wonder how the guys are doing in there?

Debbie: I'm sure they're fine. *(pauses, all start laughing hysterically)*

Leah: They are toast.

Debbie: That's for sure.

Mary: Oh wait, somebody's coming out.

(A door opens and the audience hears Joel shouting over a bunch of screaming children.)

Joel: Get off me! Help! Somebody help me! No! I do *not* want to play *horsey* again! *(the door slams and the screaming stops, Joel enters stage left looking torn apart, then crosses to Debbie and begins to cry pitifully)* What was I thinking? It was horrible! And there were so many of them. When I walked into the room this morning I could see the crazed look in their eyes. They started chanting, "fresh meat, fresh meat, fresh meat." I tried to escape but the teacher just locked the door and started laughing maniacally. And they were so hyper! They gave them punch and cookies, are those people insane? Why do they do that? Take me home ... please!

Debbie: *(hands coat to Joel who immediately holds it like a blanket and begins to suck his thumb; puts her arm around his shoulder and they begin to exit stage right)* It's okay, Joel, honey, it's all over now. *(they exit)*

Mary: Wow.

24

Leah: I know. I hope Hank is okay. If they could do that to Joel, then Hank didn't stand a chance.

(Screaming is heard offstage again along with the opening and closing of the door. Hank enters stage left, crawling and looking a lot like Joel. Hank crawls to Leah.)

Hank: Please take me home. *(reaches up and grabs Leah's leg)* Please take me home!

(Both exit stage left, Hank crawling as Leah follows him.)

Mary: *(looking very worried)* Oh, Lord, please let David at least be alive.

(The door opens offstage, but there is no screaming.)

David: *(offstage)* Good-bye, guys! I had a great time! *(door closes and David enters stage left and crosses to Mary who is looking at him suspiciously)* Hi.

Mary: Hi ... are you ... okay?

David: Of course, I had a great time in there today. I can't believe I've never done this before.

Mary: Oh, honey, they did something to you didn't they? You're delusional. Did they put something in your punch at snack time?

David: What are you talking about?

Mary: You said you had a great time.

David: That's right.

Mary: In the nursery?

David: That's right. *(Mary feels his forehead checking for a fever)* Mary, I'm fine.

Mary: But I just saw Hank and Joel come out of there, and they looked like they had just gotten out of a blender set on frappe.

David: Yeah, they had a little trouble in there today. The kids were pretty wild, especially after they got all that sugar. Why do they give them cookies and punch anyway?

Mary: I have no idea. Why the different reactions? Hank and Joel hated it and you come out talking like it was a wonderful experience.

David: Hank and Joel hated it because they were expecting to hate it from the start. I had been looking forward to this all week.

Mary: You were?

David: Sure. The pastor was right, there is a lot of joy in serving someone else, and those nursery workers needed a break. Big time. You should have seen their faces when we showed up this morning. Janice, the head teacher, hasn't been to a morning service in years. She was so happy she laughed all the way out the door. And the kids were ready for a change, too. That's probably why they were so wired. But it was fun. In fact, I signed up to work again next month, too.

Mary: Wow! I mean ... wow!

David: It's not really a big deal. It's just the way you look at it.

(Mary and David exit stage right and Narrator enters)

Narrator: One experience, three different men, three different reactions. It's amazing what you learn about service, humility, attitude, and even yourself in ... The Nursery Zone.

Blackout

26

Real Faith

Cast
   Kathy: *A housewife who is looking for some real answers*
   Brenda: *A friend*
   Carol: *Another friend*

Props
   A small kitchen table, three chairs, three cups of coffee, a plate of muffins, and three Bibles

Costumes
   Modern

―――――――――

(Lights come up on Kathy, Brenda, and Carol sitting around a kitchen table drinking coffee and eating muffins. They have their Bibles open, and are getting ready to start their weekly Bible study.)

Brenda: I'm so glad the two of you could make it this morning. I know how tough it is to get out of the house early, while trying to get your husband off to work and the kids off to school.

Carol: That's the truth. But it's worth it. I don't think I could make it through my week without this Bible study.

Kathy: *(quietly)* Me, either.

Brenda: How are things going in the Miller household, Carol?

Carol: Wonderful. Mike just got a promotion.

Brenda: Wonderful!

Kathy: *(sighs)* Good for Mike.

Carol: And little Mikey was picked for the all-star little league team. And, of course, Sally is first-chair saxophone in the band and captain of the drama team this year.

Brenda: That's wonderful, Carol. Kathy, don't you think that's wonderful?

Kathy: *(deadpan)* Wonderful.

Carol: What about you, Brenda? How's life treating you?

Brenda: Me? Well, let's see. Kyle is top salesman again this year; which means we'll be getting that big bonus again.

Carol: Last year's bonus is sitting out in the driveway right now.

Kathy: I think I took the side mirror off your bonus when I pulled in this morning.

Brenda: *(not hearing Kathy)* Sam is making straight As so far and Greg is captain of the wrestling team.

Carol: That's wonderful, Brenda. Kathy, don't you think that's wonderful?

Kathy: *(deadpan)* Wonderful.

Brenda and Carol: *(to Kathy)* What about you?

Kathy: *(long pause as she looks at the two of them)* Fine ... everything's fine.

Brenda: Are you ... sure?

Kathy: I'm sure.

Carol: Kathy, we know you, and something is obviously wrong. Don't you want to talk about it?

Kathy: *(pauses)* No ... I'm fine.

Carol: You're sure?

Kathy: Positive.

Brenda: *(pauses, unsure)* Okay then, I guess we'll get started. Okay ... our passage today is Romans 8, verse 28. *(reading)* For all things work together for good *(Kathy puts her hands in her face)* for those who are called according to his purpose. *(pauses)* Kathy? Kathy, honey, are you okay? What's wrong?

Kathy: Everything! *Everything* is wrong!

Carol: Tell us what's going on. What can we do to help?

Kathy: John was passed up for promotion again this year. He works so hard and yet he never seems to get ahead. They always promote the younger guys with the college degrees. Who cares about experience, right? So, to make up for it, he has to work longer hours just for us to make ends meet every month. I told him that I would get a job but he refused.

John, Jr. has started hanging out with some really rough kids at school and it's starting to affect his grades, his attitude, everything! I don't even know who he is anymore. When I tried to talk to him about it, he just slammed his bedroom door in my face. It was so hateful. *(starts sobbing)*

Brenda: What can we do to help?

Carol: Please tell us.

Kathy: Nothing. Nothing really. I know you want to help, but this is obviously something that you don't understand and that God doesn't care about.

Brenda: What do you mean God doesn't care? Of course he cares.

Kathy: Really? Then why is it that everything works together for good for other people and not for me? Why is it that the two of you have perfect lives and mine is one disaster after another? Everything does *not* work together for good! If it did, then my life wouldn't be such a mess.

Brenda: *(long pause)* My life isn't perfect.

Kathy: Yeah, right.

Brenda: It's true. My husband gets top salesman every year because he spends most of his year on the road. I think he keeps buying me new cars with his bonuses because he feels guilty for being gone so much. *(pauses)* I wish he'd realize that I'd rather have him.

Carol: And whose teenagers aren't difficult?

Brenda: Boy, that's the truth. Ever since Greg turned fourteen he absolutely refuses to be seen in public with me.

Carol: Sally's the same way.

Kathy: *(long pause)* I'm sorry. I didn't mean to get the two of you upset, and I didn't want to dump all of my problems on you. I just ... I just want some answers ... some *real* answers.

Carol: We all want answers. We all want faith that works in real life. My grandmother used to say that faith was no good unless it wore working clothes.

Brenda: And God *does* care.

Kathy: I know God cares. I do. It just gets so overwhelming sometimes that my problems seem bigger than he is.

Brenda: I know how you feel.

Carol: We just have to remember that when we are at our weakest, that is when he is the strongest in our lives.

Kathy: I need him to be strong in my life right now.

Brenda: *(grabbing Kathy's hand)* We all do.

Blackout

Just Like Peter

Cast
Everyman: *A middle-aged businessman*
Peter: *An offstage voice*
Jesus: *An offstage voice*

Props
A Bible and a chair

Costumes
A business suit

(There is a chair center stage. Everyman is sitting in the chair reading a Bible. He begins reading from Matthew 26:69-75.)

Everyman: *(reading)* Now Peter was sitting out in the courtyard, and a servant girl came to him. "You also were with Jesus of Galilee," she said. But he denied it before them all. "I don't know what you're talking about," he said. Then he went out to the gateway, where another girl saw him and said to the people there, "This fellow was with Jesus of Nazareth." He denied it again with an oath: "I don't know the man!" After a little while, those standing there went up to Peter and said, "Surely you are one of them, for your accent gives you away." Then he began to call down curses on himself and swore to them, "I don't know the man!" Immediately a rooster crowed. Then Peter remembered the word Jesus had spoken: "Before the rooster crows, you will disown me three times." And Peter went outside and wept bitterly.

(pauses as he considers the words he has just read) I don't know about anybody else, but I think Peter was a no good coward. I can't believe that he would stand there and deny that he even knew Jesus. After all they had been through together? He even told Jesus that he would stand by him, but when the pressure was

on, he choked! Just when Jesus needed him the most, he tucked his tail between his legs and ran. Thank God I've always stayed committed, no matter who or what has challenged me, I've stayed true to Jesus through it all.

(pauses a moment as he begins to think) I guess there was that time when my manager and a couple of his bosses went out for drinks after work and they invited me to go along. Sure I kicked back a few, but it's like I told them, the Bible just says don't get drunk. It doesn't say don't drink at all! *(laughs, but it fades quickly)*

Of course Doug Watson heard that I had gone. I had been witnessing to him for three years, but after that night, he refused to even talk to me about God. He never said anything, but I knew what he was thinking. He thought I was a hypocrite.

(brief pause) But that wasn't *denying* Christ. How was I supposed to know the guy was going to be offended, besides the fact that we are talking about my career here, and sometimes you have to do certain things to get ahead, and when the boss asks you to go out, you do it, you can't fault me for that, right? I know nobody wants some Bible thumping Christian fanatic as a district manager. I had to show him I was just like everybody else.

At least I never dishonored God in front of my family. At least my wife and kids have always known where I stand.

(pauses) Okay, okay, so maybe my kids have seen me watch some movies that I probably shouldn't have watched. It's not like they were rated X or anything, just rated R. You know, just good old-fashioned action flicks. I told them that they were too young and innocent to watch stuff like that because of the bad language and the violence. They asked me when I had stopped being young ... and innocent.

(pauses as conviction begins to weigh heavily on him) I guess it hasn't been any different with the folks at church, either. A lot of my friends have heard me complaining about some of things the pastor has been implementing lately. I guess I haven't really supported him like I should and I may have made a little trouble for him, but ... I had a good reason ... I just didn't agree with what he was doing ... and ... I ...

(picks up the Bible and looks at it, then throws it back down again) This is ridiculous. I'm making myself feel guilty for nothing. What am I supposed to be, some kind of super Christian, some kind of saint? I'm just like everybody else. I'm just like ... *(looks at Bible)* I'm just like Peter. *(breaks, falls to his knees, and begins to weep ... bitterly)* Forgive me Lord ... forgive me Lord.

Jesus: *(offstage)* Simon, son of John, do you truly love me more than these?

Peter: *(offstage)* Yes, Lord, you know that I love you.

Jesus: Feed my lambs. *(pauses)* Simon, son of John, do you truly love me?

Peter: Yes, Lord, you know that I love you.

Jesus: Take care of my sheep. *(pauses)* Simon, son of John, do you love me?

Peter: Lord, you know all things; you know that I love you.

Jesus: Feed my sheep.

Everyman: *(looks up to heaven)* Lord, you know that I love you.

Blackout

The Faith Bridge

Cast
　Waiter: *A man or woman*
　Walker: *A man or woman*

Props
　A chair

Costumes
　Modern

———————

(Waiter is sitting in a chair facing stage left. He is dozing off, looking rather bored. He jerks himself awake, stands up and looks at the ground a couple of feet in front of him. He shakes his head in disgust, goes back to his chair, sits down and is soon fast asleep and snoring loudly. Walker enters stage right and walks past Waiter a couple of feet, which should put him at about center stage. Walker stops, looks down at the ground for a moment and then shakes his head as if he is confused. Walker then looks at Waiter and speaks.)

Walker: Excuse me. *(Waiter is still asleep)* Excuse me!

Waiter: *(startled)* No, I didn't! Yes, I will! *(now fully awake)* Oh ... sorry.

Walker: I'm sorry to wake you, but I was wondering if there was another place to cross this gorge. There's no bridge here.

Waiter: Nope. There is no other place to cross. Believe me, I've checked. I've checked 100 times, this is it.

Walker: I don't get it. I know God told me to come this way. He told me to cross this gorge at this spot, but there's no bridge. How am I supposed to get across?

Waiter: Welcome to Christianity, pal. God told me the same thing three years ago. I came to the spot where you are standing and I asked myself the exact same question. I've looked all around this side of the gorge. It never ends and there is no other place to cross.

Walker: So what did you do?

Waiter: I decided to wait. If God wants me to cross here, then he's gonna have to build a bridge.

Walker: You've been sitting here waiting for God to build a bridge for three years?

Waiter: Yep. You see, I've got faith. I believe that when it's time for me to cross, God will make a way. Until then, it's my job to trust him.

Walker: What about obeying him?

Waiter: Huh?

Walker: It seems to me that if God wanted us to cross here, there would have to be some way.

Waiter: Look. *(crosses to Walker)* Do you see the bottom of that gorge?

Walker: No.

Waiter: Exactly! Now do you think I'm going to step off this nice solid ground here into thin air and just trust God? That's crazy!

Walker: I thought stepping off into thin air and trusting God was faith.

Waiter: Okay, fine. If that's what you want to do, go right ahead. If you want to be a fanatic and refuse to listen to someone who has been here three years ahead of you, then don't let me keep you from the bottom of the gorge.

Walker: But you've been here for three years doing nothing when you know what God told you to do. That's not maturity, that's stagnation.

Waiter: *(has no response, looks into the gorge, shakes his head, and returns to his seat)* I can't, I just can't.

Walker: *(turns and stands on the edge of the gorge)* Lord, I'm here because you told me to cross this gorge, and you told me to do it now. Therefore, you must have made a way. I trust you. *(closes his eyes and takes a step forward; Waiter hides his eyes waiting on him to scream then turns to look when he hears Walker talking excitedly)* Look at this! It's a bridge! God made it right under my feet! This is amazing. I knew I could trust you, Lord. *(Walker waves good-bye and walks across the stage, then exits)*

Waiter: *(stands and shakes his head in disbelief)* I don't believe it. He was right. God really did make a way. *(looks back down at the gorge in confusion)* Wait a minute! Where did the bridge go? How am I supposed to get across? *(steps up to the edge of gorge, takes a deep breath, and sticks his leg out as if he is going to step off, then he suddenly jerks himself back)* What am I, nuts? Faith is one thing, but there is no way I'm stepping off that cliff when I can't see my way across. *(goes back to his chair, sits down, and is soon fast asleep again)*

Blackout

39

All Too Important

Cast
Jim: *A busy man*
Karen: *Jim's wife*

Props
A Bible, a golf club, a serving spoon, a checkbook, a brief-case, a baseball glove, a table, and a rake

Costumes
Jim is dressed for work, and Karen is dressed for church.

(Lights come up with Jim standing center stage adjusting his tie. To his left is a table with the various props used in the sketch. The Bible should be at the bottom of the pile. Karen enters stage right and crosses to stand beside Jim.)

Karen: I'm ready.

Jim: Ready for what?

Karen: For church. Jim, you do remember that it's Sunday?

Jim: Karen I can't go to church, I have to work.

Karen: Work? On a Sunday?

Jim: Honey, how am I ever going to get that promotion I want if I don't put in the extra hours on weekends? *(picks up the briefcase)*

Karen: But we really need to go to ...

Jim: Little Jimmy's baseball game? Don't worry, honey, I won't forget that. *(picks up the baseball glove)*

41

Karen: I wasn't talking about the game, I was talking about ...

Jim: The grounds committee meeting? I've got it covered. *(picks up the rake)*

Karen: Jim, you really need to ...

Jim: Serve in the community more? I know it's good business. That's why I signed up to serve in the city soup kitchen once a week. *(picks up the serving spoon)*

Karen: You're working in a soup kitchen? When is that going to leave time for ...

Jim: For you? Karen, don't you think you're being just a little bit selfish here? I'm doing the best that I can. *(Karen starts to speak, but Jim cuts her off)* Okay, okay, I'll take you to dinner later this week, I promise. *(picks up the checkbook)* Happy?

Karen: No Jim, when are you going to have time for ...

Jim: Oh, you mean when am I going to have time for myself? Thank you honey, that's so thoughtful of you. *(picks up the golf club)* I'll go play golf next Sunday, I promise.

Karen: *(forceful)* No, Jim, I'm not talking about golf. I'm talking about God. When are you going to have time to go to church? When are you going to take time to read your Bible or pray? When are you going to give time to him? *(There is a pause as Jim looks down at the table where the Bible is sitting. He tries picking it up several times but with no success. He looks back at Karen.)* It looks like you're going to have to let something go, dear.

Jim: *(pulls all of his things close to him)* I can't let any of this go ... it's all too important.

Blackout

42

Remember Me

Cast
Player: *A man or woman*

Props
None

Costumes
Be creative. You can use stylistic, biblical, or modern.

Production Notes
This monologue is designed to produce a worshipful mood as your congregation prepares to take communion. Anything you can do to enhance the environment such as dimmed lighting or soft music will only add to the worship experience.

———————

(As the lights come up and the music is playing, Player stands center stage with his head bowed. When ready, Player will slowly raise his head, look at the audience for a moment and begin. The monologue should be delivered with great depth of emotion.)

Player: Remember when I told you that I loved you? You heard it in my voice, you saw it in my eyes, and you felt it in my touch. Remember that I love you still.

Remember when I laid my hands on you and healed you? I took away the darkness, I banished your sickness, and I brought strength to your body. Remember that I heal you still.

Remember when I opened my mouth and gave you the words of life? I nourished your soul and brought life to your spirit. Remember that I feed you still.

Remember when I was beaten, broken, and mocked? The nails pierced my hands and feet. I took your sins on myself, and I carried your cross. Remember, I forgive you still.

Remember when I was laid in the tomb and left as dead? For three days I laid in the belly of the earth.

Remember when I left that tomb ... alive! Death defeated, life everlasting given to you. Remember, I give you life still.

Remember me when you take this bread. Remember me when you take this cup. Remember ... remember me.

Blackout

A Sparrow Falls

Cast

    Bob: *A homeless man*

Props

    An overturned garbage can with trash flowing out of it and a park bench

Costumes

    Bob is a homeless man. He should look the part.

(Bob enters as the lights come up. He crosses to the overturned garbage can and looks down at in disgust.)

Bob: Look at this. People got no respect for anything anymore. Do I go over to other people's houses and throw garbage all over their living room floor? I don't think so. *(picks up the garbage can and sees something of interest in it; begins to pull items out of the can and throw them on the floor; then, to the audience)* It's my house. I can put garbage on the floor if I want to. *(finds some left-over food, sniffs it, and takes a bite)* A guy's gotta eat, right? *(digs some more and finds a bottle of alcohol with a little left in the bottom)* Jackpot! Come to daddy you gorgeous thing you. Oh, yeah! *(looks at the bottle)* Hmm, a very good year. *(takes sniff)* Delightful bouquet, good color ... bottoms up! *(takes a drink)* Yow! Has that got a kick! Nasty! Just nasty! This stuff would put hair on your eyeballs. No self-respecting wino would let this poison past his lips more than once. Guess it's a good thing I don't fit into that category. *(Takes another drink, gathers some newspapers lying around, and starts to lay down on the bench, covering himself with the newspapers. Just as soon as he gets comfortable and closes his eyes, singing of hymns is heard offstage.)*

    No, no, not again! Can't you people give it a rest for one night! I'm trying to get my beauty sleep! *(laughs at his own joke)* Beauty sleep, that's a good one. *(tries to get comfortable again, but the*

45

singing continues; after a few moments, he jumps up and stands beside the bench shouting off stage right) I said shut up! Every single night it's the same thing. It's getting so a guy can't even get sloppy drunk and pass out without some Bible thumping group of mission going, hymn singing, verse quoting, do-good-Christians disrupting his stupor. What's the world coming to anyway?

(turns and looks at the audience) Hey there, pal, you gotta buck you can spare? Come on, pal, one dollar. You're a wealthy guy, I can tell by that fancy watch your wearing. Hey, whoa, I'm not gonna try and rob you, calm down. I just want a dollar. What? No, I haven't been drinking, I don't drink, drinking will kill you. *(pauses)* Oh ... this? *(indicates bottle)* This is um ... cough medicine. Yeah, for my sick grandmother. The poor old thing has been hacking up a lung since Thursday and she needs to get her sleep, so I got her some really strong cough medicine to help her out you know? *(pauses)* You're not buying this one, huh? Yeah, that was a pretty lousy performance. I wouldn't give myself a dollar for that one.

So I drink. What business is that of yours anyway? What do you care? Like you're some kind of saint or something like that? You never touch the stuff? Who cares? What's left in this bottle ought to keep me company for the night and I can practice my story for the next guy that comes by here lost. How do I know you're lost? Please ... look at yourself ... look at where you are ... it's dark, you're in the worst part of the city, and you're dressed like you just stepped out of *GQ* magazine! It's obvious you're in the wrong place.

(pauses) You want me to give you directions? Look at me, pal, I'm an alcoholic, unemployed bum living on the streets eating out of a garbage can and drinking what tastes like mouthwash that's past its expiration date, and I know what that tastes like. Does that sound like somebody you want to take directions from? I don't think so. Besides, you wouldn't give me a lousy dollar and now you want me to do something for you? What color is the sky in your world buddy? Because that is not the way it works out here. Where are you going anyway? *(pauses)* The street mission? Of all the lousy no good ... that's all I need is one more Bible thumper

46

adding to the racket over there. Can you not see that giant blue neon sign right down the street that says "Jesus Saves"? Yeah, that's the mission. *(pauses)* Yeah, you're welcome.

What do you want to go there for anyway? It's just a bunch of losers. Not that I'm not a loser, too, but at least I'm not so weak and pathetic that I need some kind of crutch to help me deal with the fact that life stinks. That's all God is anyway, a crutch. God is just a way for weak-minded people to deal with all the pain in the world without going crazy.

For instance, do I come crying to God when I'm freezing to death in the middle of the winter with nothing between me and the cold but a few newspapers and a tattered old coat? I don't think so. I button up my coat a little tighter and I make it through ... without God's help. Do I come crying to God when I haven't eaten in three days and I'm digging through trashcans trying to find some half-eaten rotten food to choke down? No! I just keep digging because I won't use a crutch.

(long pause with building emotion) And did I come crying to God when my young, beautiful wife died because she was hit head-on by some truck driver who had fallen asleep at the wheel? She was so young, and so beautiful. She had so much to offer the world. And then ... she was gone. In a second she was gone! And I was alone. But did I whine to God? No, no! I didn't because I don't need God. I didn't because God is not real. There is no God! At least no God I want to know.

What kind of a God would take my wife from me? Can you answer that one? Please, can you at least tell me that? If God is responsible for this world, then don't go to that mission. You just stay lost. Just stay lost. That's what I'm going to do. I'm staying lost.

(goes back to the bench and sits down, there is a pause and he looks up) Why are you still here? You what? You want me to go with you to the mission? You think I'll find some answers there, huh? I don't think so. Why? After everything I just said you ask me, "Why?" What's the point, pal? I need a God that makes sense, and your God doesn't make sense to me. Besides, they're loud enough I can hear them from here. Thanks anyway. *(pauses as he looks toward the mission; then he looks up to heaven)*

47

God. Or whatever you're called up there. People say that you are love. They say that you provide, that you care. My mother used to say that not even a sparrow falls to the ground without you noticing. What does that make me, God? Because I fell a long time ago, and you never seemed to notice. I didn't just fall, I got run over in the middle of the street and you didn't notice. That's me, sparrow roadkill.

(singing from the mission begins again and he looks in the direction of the sound and begins to cry) God, you sound so real to them in there. Why can't you be real to us out here?

Blackout

The Thanksgiving Tradition

Cast

Joey: *A lovable guy from the Bronx (should be played with a thick accent)*

Props

None

Costumes

Jeans, T-shirts, sneakers, and a ball cap worn backward

Production Notes

This monologue is written so that it can be performed the Sunday *after* Thanksgiving, but with slight alterations, it can be performed earlier.

A word should also be said about the character of Joey. No matter where I have performed this monologue, people always love this character. He should be played as a real salt of the earth kind of guy that everybody knows. As an actor, you have a real opportunity to create a memorable person that takes on a life of his own. Develop your own pattern of speech and mannerisms that will bring real life to Joey. Your audience will respond according to how "real" you can make him.

———————

(Joey enters stage right and crosses to center stage. He should be speaking as he walks.)

Joey: Hey, how you folks doin'? Everybody doin' all right and all? Yeah? Good. Did you have a good Thanksgiving? Yeah? Did you eat a lot of turkey and spend time with your family and all that? Yeah, me too.

Me and my family all go out to my ma and pop's house for Thanksgiving every year. My ma cooks like this huge dinner and we stuff ourselves like pigs all day long. Then we all take enough food home with us to last until next spring, you know what I'm sayin'?

And talk about relatives. Forget about it. There's like a million people at these things and most of 'em I only see once a year, so I don't even know who they are. And they're all coming up to me and pinching my cheeks and I'm thinking *hey, back off, pal, 'cause I don't know you and I'm real particular about who pinches these babies, all right?*

So anyway, this year I ask my ma, I say, "Hey, Ma, how come we gotta have all these people over here every year?" And she says *(imitating his mother)*, "Joey, you're supposed to have family over on Thanksgiving, it's tradition."

So I started thinking about it, and I'm thinking *yeah, that makes sense to me, my family's got a lot of traditions.*

For instance, there's my grandpa Joey, my little cousin Joey, and my uncle Joey. They got this tradition of watching football every year. And they couldn't pick a winner if their lives depended on it, you know what I'm sayin'?

Then there's my aunt Roberta. She's got this tradition of making this sweet potato soufflé every year. And that's one tradition we could all live without, you know what I'm sayin'? She's got a good heart and all, but she's no Martha Stewart, if you know what I mean.

And she's always trying to get everybody to eat more of it, too. She's got this real raspy voice and she's like *(imitating Roberta)*, "Joey, you're a growing boy, eat some more soufflé." And I'm thinking, *yeah, Roberta, and I want to stay that way, all right?* Forget about it. Two helpings of that stuff will permanently stunt you're growth.

My pop has this tradition of carving up the bird every year. Did I say carve? Forget about it. He just kind hacks at that poor thing like he's got some kind of Bruce Lee thing going on.

Then there's my cousin Louisa whose tradition is bringing her fiancé to dinner every year. They've been engaged for like eight years, nobody in the family thinks they are actually gonna get married.

Then there's my ma who makes the big dinner, and then there's me. And when I started thinking about it I realized that I didn't really have any Thanksgiving tradition so you know what I decided? I decided that my tradition was going to be thanksgiving. Now I'm not talking about with the turkey and the football and the fiancé and the sweet potato soufflé. I'm talking about having thanksgiving in my heart to God for all the great stuff he's done for us. And I'm not talking about once a year, either. God has done so much for us we should be celebrating Thanksgiving every day. So I thought, *yeah, that's my tradition.*

It's been real nice talking to you folks, but if you'll excuse me, I gotta figure out what I'm gonna do with ten pounds of Roberta's soufflé. *(pauses)* Anybody need a driveway repaved?

Blackout

Joey, The Wise Guy

Cast
> Joey: *A lovable guy from the Bronx (should be played with a thick accent)*

Props
> None

Costumes
> Jeans, T-shirt, sneakers, and a ball cap worn backward

Production Note
> This monologue is written for performance the Sunday *after* Christmas, but with some slight alterations, it can be performed earlier.

(Joey enters stage right and crosses to center stage. He should be speaking as he walks.)

Joey: Hey, how you folks doin' tonight? Did you have a good Christmas? Did you celebrate it right? You know with the tree and the presents and all that? Yeah, me too.

Yeah, we had a good Christmas this year. But I gotta tell you this story, you're gonna love this. It was like the coolest and the weirdest thing I've ever heard about happening at Christmas.

Okay, here it goes. My aunt Roberta was put in charge of the Christmas program at her church this year ... big mistake! She's got a good heart and all, but Roberta is like the queen of the Broadway musical, you know what I sayin'? She can't do some nice little show about the baby Jesus bein' born and all, she's got to make this huge production. For example, last year for Easter she puts this thing on and it's like phantom of the opera meets the disciples at the resurrection or some kinda thing. It was like, for-

53

get about it, nobody knew what that one was about.

So anyway, she does this Christmas thing and it was some story about Santa Claus and he's makin' his rounds on Christmas Eve and all of a sudden this big snowstorm comes up and blows him off course. He ends up in Bethlehem and finds the baby Jesus right after he was born. Now this part is still a little fuzzy, but somewhere along the way he picks up Scrooge, Danny Kaye, and Bing Crosby ... forget about it.

So I show up on the night of the performance because she's family and all that, when all of a sudden my aunt Roberta comes running up to me in tears. Her hair's all messed up and her makeup is running all over the place, it was kinda scary, you know what I'm sayin'?

She comes up to me and says *(imitating Roberta)*, "Joey, you gotta help me, it's a disaster." I finally get her calmed down enough to tell me that one of her wise guys came down with the flu and can't make it. So now, she only has two wise guys to give the baby Jesus all this stuff that they brought. You know, all the gold and Frankenstein and what was the other thing? Nutmeg or something, I don't know. Anyway, she wants to know if I'll play one of the wise guys for her. So I says, "Yeah, sure, Roberta, I'll be one of the wise guys." After all, she's my mother's sister, what am I gonna say, "No"? Forget about it.

Now I know what you're thinkin'. You're thinkin', *Joey, it's wise* men, *not wise* guys. Yeah, well you've never been to my neighborhood, you know what I'm sayin'?

So I get into costume and all that and the show starts and it's like this really huge deal because ... that's my aunt Roberta. Let's see, we got Danny Kaye tap dancing to "White Christmas." We got Bing Crosby singing *(sings like Bing Crosby)*, "You must have been a Bethlehem baby," and we got eight tiny reindeer, who were actually my cousins dressed up in weird costumes, all running around making all kinds of racket.

The show's going along fine when all of a sudden, one of the reindeer, I think it was my cousin Joey, bumps into Danny Kaye during one of his routines. Danny loses his balance and falls back into the platform that the Christmas angel is standing on. The Christmas angel starts to fall off the platform, so she grabs hold of the Christmas star, which is hanging on this flimsy curtain. The curtain rips and the platform, the angel, and the star come crashing down and take out Danny Kaye and two of the reindeer. The whole set then comes crashing down into one great big pile of Christmas, my aunt Roberta passes out on the front row, and everybody in the audience is looking at me ... cause I'm the only one left standing. I looked around ... and I started to get a little embarrassed. Not because everybody was looking at me, but because we had made such a mess of Jesus' birthday. In fact, I felt so bad I started to pray. *(takes off his hat and looks up)*

Jesus, I'm sorry we made such a mess out of your birthday and all. I guess sometimes we get so caught up in Christmas we forget to make sure you're a part of it. I want you to know that we sure are glad you were born and all because if you hadn't come along, none of us would be here. I'm sorry Jesus but I promise ... we'll do better next year.

After I finished praying, the pastor comes up to me and says, "Joey, you're a really wise man." I said, "Naaah *(puts his hat back on)*, I'm just a wise guy."

Blackout

The Christmas Story

Cast
> Reader 1: *A man or woman*
> Reader 2: *A man*
> Reader 3: *A woman*
> Reader 4: *A man or woman*

Props
> None

Costumes
> Modern

Production Notes

In this reading, Reader 1 will primarily be the narrator, Reader 2 will serve as the voice for the male characters, Reader 3 will serve as the voice of the female characters, and Reader 4 will serve as the prophetic voice. This reading is best done with accompanying music and should be delivered in a somewhat rapid manner while still maintaining the worshipful tone of the piece.

Reader 1: In the beginning, before all time, was the word.

Reader 2: And the word was with God.

Reader 3: And the word was God.

Reader 4: He was with God ... in the beginning.

Reader 1: All things were made and came into existence through him; and without him was not even one thing made that has come into being.

Reader 2: In him was life and the life was the light of men.

Reader 4: The people walking in darkness have seen a great light, on those living in the land of the shadow of death a light has dawned.

Reader 3: And the light shines in the darkness, for the darkness has never overpowered it. *(pauses)* This is how the birth of Jesus came about.

Reader 1: God sent the angel Gabriel to Nazareth, to a town in Galilee, to a virgin pledged to be married to a man named Joseph, a descendant of David. The virgin's name ... was Mary.

Reader 4: The Lord himself will give you a sign. The virgin will be with child and will give birth to a son, and will call him Immanuel.

Reader 1: The angel went to her and said ...

Reader 2: Greetings, you who are highly favored, the Lord is with you.

Reader 1: But when she saw him, she was greatly troubled and wondered what such a greeting might mean.

Reader 2: Do not be afraid, Mary, you have found favor with God. You will be with child and give birth to a son, and you are to give him the name, Jesus.

Reader 3: Wonderful Counselor.

Reader 4: Mighty God.

Reader 1: Everlasting Father *(pauses)* Prince of Peace.

Reader 2: The Lord God will give him the throne of his father David, and he will reign ...

Reader 4: For unto us a child is born, unto us a son is given, and the government will be upon his shoulders, of the increase of his government there will be no end. He was given authority, glory, and sovereign power, all peoples, nations and men of every language worshiped him.

All: His dominion is an everlasting dominion that will not pass away.

Reader 4: And his kingdom is one that will never be destroyed.

Reader 3: How will this be since I am a virgin?

Reader 2: The Holy Spirit will come upon you, and the power of the Most High will overshadow you. So the holy one to be born will be called the Son of God.

Reader 3: I am the Lord's servant, may it be done to me as you have said.

Reader 1: In those days Caesar Augustus issued a decree that a census should be taken of the entire Roman world.

Reader 2: So Joseph also went up from the town of Nazareth to Bethlehem, the town of David, because he belonged to the house and lineage of David.

Reader 4: But you, Bethlehem, though you are small among the clans of Judah, out of you will come for me one who will be ruler over Israel, whose origins are from old, from ancient times.

Reader 2: Joseph went there to register with Mary who was pledged to be married to him and was expecting a child.

Reader 1: While they were there, the time came for the baby to be born.

Reader 3: And she gave birth to her firstborn, a son. She wrapped him in cloths, and placed him in a manger,

Reader 2: because there was no room for them in the inn.

Reader 1: And there were shepherds living out in the fields nearby, keeping watch over their flocks by night. An angel of the Lord appeared to them, and the glory of the Lord shone around them, and they were terrified.

Reader 3: But the angel said ...

Reader 2: Do not be afraid. I bring you good news of great joy

Reader 3: which will be for all people.

Reader 2: Today in the town of David

Reader 1: a Savior has been born to you;

Reader 4: he is Christ the Lord!

All: Christ the Lord!

Reader 3: This will be a sign to you:

Reader 2: You will find the baby wrapped in cloths and lying in a manger.

Reader 1: Suddenly a great company of the heavenly host appeared with the angel, praising God and saying,

All: Glory to God in the highest, and on earth peace to men on whom his favor rests!

Reader 1: When the angels had left them and gone into heaven, the shepherds said to one another,

Reader 2: Let's go to Bethlehem and see this thing that has happened.

Reader 3: So they hurried off and found Mary ...

Reader 2: and Joseph ...

Reader 1: and the baby, lying in a manger.

Reader 2: When they had seen him, they spread the word!

Reader 3: They told everyone.

Reader 1: Everyone.

Reader 2: What had been told to them about this child.

Reader 4: For my eyes have seen your salvation, which you have prepared in the sight of all people, a light for revelation to the Gentiles and glory to your people Israel.

Reader 1: The Word became flesh and made his dwelling among us.

Reader 2: We have seen his glory, the glory of the One and Only,

Reader 4: who came from the Father, full of grace and truth.

Blackout

David's First Christmas

Cast
    David: *A shepherd*

Props
    A staff

Costumes
    Modern dress, preferably jeans and a flannel shirt

David: *(to audience)* Hey, you, come here. Come over here, I have got to tell you something. *(pauses)* He's here. *(snickers)* No really, it's true ... he's here, he's right here in Bethlehem. Actually he's more like *(pointing)* over there in Bethlehem. *(pauses)* Who? Whadda ya mean who? Who do you think? The Messiah! Didn't you see the angels with all of the music and the lights and ... Oh, I guess you missed that huh? Okay, here it goes. I'm gonna tell you a story and when I'm finished you are probably going to call me a liar to my face, but I'm telling you, it's the truth.

Oh, by the way, my name's David *(pauses)*, as in King David. *(pauses)* Well, no, obviously not *the* King David, he's been dead for like ... well ... a really long time. I'm just named after him. But I'm also from Bethlehem and I'm a shepherd so that means we are like this. *(crosses his fingers)*

All the guys, they make fun of me they call me, "Your Majesty," and what not. I walk up and they start bowing and all that. It's a little embarrassing at first, but you get used to it.

Anyway, we were all out in the pasture watching the sheep because that's what we do ... we're shepherds. We were just shootin' the breeze and all because watching sheep can get pretty boring, if you know what I mean. I always thought it would be cool to be like a lion herder, or something like that, but sheep don't really do that much. In fact, sometimes when I have to count them, I just fall asleep. It's the weirdest thing.

We were all hanging out with the sheep when all of a sudden ... bam! This light comes flashing out of the sky and this giant bright dude with wings coming out of his back is floating right above our heads. He was so cool looking, and pretty scary, if you ask me. In fact, I was terrified. Then he spoke *(speaks in a deep voice when he is quoting the angel)*: "Do not be afraid." And I'm thinking, *yeah, right! Have you looked at yourself lately?* But he goes on: "I bring you good news of great joy that will be for all people." And I'm like, good! Because after the way you just scared the sandals off me, I could use some good news. "Today, in the town of David, a Savior has been born to you; he is Christ the Lord."

And I'm thinking ... *this is so ... awesome! A savior, in my hometown! Nothing, and I mean nothing ever happens in Bethlehem.* But he wasn't finished: "This will be a sign to you. You will find a baby wrapped in cloths and lying in a manger."

A manger? Now that's really weird. What kind of parents does this kid have anyway? Putting a little baby in a food trough? I thought I had it rough.

But if all that weren't enough, all of a sudden ... bam! The sky splits open and as far as the eye can see there were these angels with the wings flying around all over the place. There was light everywhere and this awesome music and they all started singing. *(sings majestically)* "Glory to God in the highest!" And boom, bam! It was all so ... cool!

After a while, they all just sort of *(pauses)* poof, disappeared. We were standing around staring at each other like *(stares with mouth wide open)*. Then Ben says *(imitating Ben)*, "Hey, you guys think we should go check this stuff out?" And I'm like, "Duh! Hello? Anybody home? You think I'm going to hang out here with some sheep when the Messiah is around?"

So we took off out of there and after awhile we found this couple staying in a barn behind a hotel. There was the mom and the dad and *(pauses, then with a sense of awe)* there he was ... just this little baby boy cooing away in a manger just like the angel said. There he was ... the Messiah.

What else could we do? *(kneels)* Thank you, Lord. Thank you. *(bows his head and pauses)* You know for hundreds of years, people had talked about how the Messiah, the King, was going to come set us free, and then here he was and I was looking at him right in the face. Me, a little nobody shepherd from a nowhere town, and I was in the presence of the King of Israel. *(long pause as he stands, then smiles)* I got to hold him. That was cool.

His parents said his name is Jesus. *(trying it out)* Jesus ... yeah that's a good name. You better remember it, you will definitely be hearing it again.

From now on, when those guys make fun of me, I won't care. I may be a nobody whose got the name of an old king, but tonight I got to see the real King of Israel. That's something special. It's a pretty special day wouldn't you say? Today, Jesus, the Messiah was born ... don't you forget it.

Blackout

The Road To Emmaus

Cast

Disciple: *One of the disciples on the road to Emmaus*

Props

None

Costumes

Biblical or modern

(Disciple enters in an excited state and crosses to center stage.)

Disciple: If you are a follower of Jesus, then listen closely to me. I have a wonderful story to tell, a story of an amazing journey and stranger who showed the way.

Cleopas and I were walking along the road that leads to Emmaus. As we walked, we spoke mainly of Jesus. We talked about his ministry, his teaching, and his power. We also talked about his death. He had been dead for three days and now it looked as if we had been wrong about him. He was not the Messiah, the deliverer of Israel.

Without so much as a word of warning, a stranger walked beside us on the road. He seemed so familiar to us, as if he had been walking beside us all along. He asked what we were talking about and so we told him about Jesus and all that had happened over the last few days. We told him about how our hopes had been destroyed with Jesus on the cross.

The stranger looked at us and with great authority he rebuked us for being slow to believe all that the prophets had spoken. Then he began with Moses and all of the prophets and explained to us from the scriptures everything concerning Jesus ... the Messiah.

As he spoke, our hearts burned within us. Listening to him was like feeding our souls with the most nourishing of foods. His teaching was like cool water satisfying a desperate thirst. We felt the same way when we would listen to Jesus.

When we reached Emmaus, we begged him to come stay with us and we were thrilled when he agreed. As we sat at the table together, the stranger took bread, gave thanks, and broke it. There was something so familiar in the way he did this. As he broke the bread, I looked and saw two scars, one on each wrist. Two scars ... two ... nail scars. Jesus? Yes, Jesus!

Immediately he disappeared from our sight. Cleopas and I danced for joy! We embraced, we cried, we laughed, and we praised God in heaven because it was true. It is true! Jesus is alive!

Blackout

Sunrise

A Play For Easter In Six Scenes

Cast

Karen: *A Christian woman who has agreed to take part in a play for an Easter sunrise service*
Sam: *Karen's husband. He is also playing a part in the play*
Mary: *The mother of Jesus*
Alexander: *A Roman soldier*
Mary Magdalene: Mary of Magdala
Peter: *The apostle*

Props

A spear, a red cloth, which will be used as a shawl for Mary, Jesus' mother's head, and a chair

Costumes

In order to make character transitions smoother, this play was originally performed with the actors dressed only in black. However, if you will be using multiple performers, a variety of costumes can be used.

Production Notes

Sunrise was first written for two performers who played all of the parts, but it can be performed by as many as six. Although the original purpose of the play was to be utilized in an Easter sunrise service, the staging and props are minimal, making it easy to use for other purposes as well.

The most important aspect of the play is that the transitions from character to character are made with no blurred lines. In other words, each character must be distinct and separate from the others.

This play is also very emotionally charged. The sound effects and stage directions will help add to the atmosphere and mood of the play. Feel free to experiment with various sound or musical effects in order to achieve the atmosphere you desire.

Scenes two, three, and five can also be played as sketches.

Running Time
20 to 25 minutes

Scene One

(It is before dawn at an Easter sunrise service. Karen is standing center stage. She is nervously practicing. The only other things on stage are a chair and a red shawl, which she is holding in her hands.)

Karen: I stand here today saying good-bye to my son, the king of glory, the Lord ... um ... the Lord ... I will never get this right. *(takes a deep breath)* I stand here today saying good morning to ... no that's not right either. What am I doing here?

Sam: *(enters from stage right, as Karen is speaking, carrying a spear; crosses to Karen as he speaks)* Those are my thoughts exactly. What in the world would get us to volunteer to be in a play?

Karen: You mean besides the drama director begging us on hands and knees with big tears streaming down her cheeks?

Sam: Oh, yeah. She should get an Oscar for that performance.

Karen: Sam, I can't do this. I'm so nervous I feel like I'm going to be sick.

Sam: Those aren't nerves, Karen, it's the fact that it is before dawn and neither one of us has had even the first cup of coffee.

Karen: I had coffee.

Sam: *(alarmed)* What? Where did you get coffee?

Karen: Over by the van. They had a table set up with coffee and doughnuts for everybody. You were trying on your costume.

Sam: *(bolts off stage but returns a moment later, empty-handed, except for the spear, then speaks to the offstage area)* Couldn't even leave a stinking cup of coffee for me, could you? *(to Karen)* Now what am I supposed to do? And I am not wearing that costume, either.

Karen: *(playfully)* Oh, come on, sweetie, you look good in a skirt.

Sam: You see, that's exactly what I'm talking about. How did the Roman army conquer the entire world wearing dresses?

Karen: Well, if you're worried about the hair on your legs you can always shave them before the performance.

Sam: That's not funny, Karen, it really isn't. That costume is an affront to my manhood, and I will not wear it.

Karen: Okay, okay, calm down. I'm just trying to lighten the mood a little. Now if you will excuse me, *I* have lines to work on.

Sam: That's one good thing about being the soldier, no lines.

Karen: Boy, did you get off easy. All you have to do is fall to the ground like a dead man when the tomb opens up.

Sam: That's right. And I have that part down cold. *(demonstrates by falling to the ground like a stone)*

Karen: Oh, bravo.

Sam: *(stands and takes a bow)* Thank you, ladies and gentlemen, thank you. No applause please just money.

Karen: Okay, enough funny stuff. I really have to work on these lines, and they aren't coming very easily.

Sam: Come on, honey. Don't be nervous, you're going to be great. You know you're the one with all the talent in the family, and the theater background.

Karen: I would hardly call playing bread in an elementary school play about the four food groups a theater background.

Sam: You're just being modest. I'm sure you were wonderful bread.

Karen: It's not that anyway, it's these lines. They seem so fake. I don't think Mary would have said all of this stuff. Her son had just died. What mother is going to stand there and boldly declare *(quoting)* "I stand here to bid farewell to my son, the Lord Jesus Christ, the King of Glory"? That's not the heart cry of a mother who has just lost her son. If I had been her, I would have been devastated.

Sam: Yeah, well, they have done the same play at every sunrise service this church has ever had. It's just the way it's done.

Karen: That doesn't make it right. These characters were real people, Sam. They had feelings and fears. The events surrounding the Easter story were some of the most terrible, frightening, and wonderful things they had ever experienced. Why can't we show that in this play?

Sam: Come on, Karen, it's just a sunrise service. We do it every year and it's never any different. It's just the same old story.

Karen: Did you hear what you just said? It is Resurrection Sunday, Sam. Have you forgotten what that means? It is *not* just the same old story.

Sam: I didn't mean anything by that ...

Karen: *(calming down)* I know, I know, and I'm not trying to be critical, I just want to be able to recapture the passion of the resurrection. The story has become old to me, too, and that scares me, Sam. What could be more important to a Christian than the resurrection?

Sam: You're right. The only thing I've been thinking about today is getting a cup of coffee and making sure I don't have to wear that soldier's costume. And I see what you mean about the play. It does seem a little ...

Karen: Old?

Sam: Yeah ... old. *(pauses thoughtfully)* Sometimes I wonder what it was *really* like for the people back then. For the ones that knew Jesus, that walked with him for three and a half years. People like Mary Magdalene and Simon Peter. I'll bet the story never got old for them. They lived it! They probably told it 1,000 times and always had the same fire in their eyes that they had the first time.

Karen: Why should that change now? Why should it be different for us than it was for them?

Sam: Maybe if we could just see it through their eyes.

Karen: *(pauses)* What *would* it have been like for the mother of Jesus? To watch your son die like that? *(Softly, music begins, or the sounds of the crucifixion as the lights begin to fade. The sounds become louder until they drown out Karen's voice and the lights have faded to black.)* What would she have felt? What would she have said or done? She must have been so heartbroken. To have watched Jesus suffer for the sins of all humankind when he was pure and innocent ...

Blackout

73

Scene Two

(The sounds of the crucifixion have ended. The lights come up on Karen who is now Mary, the mother of Jesus. She is wearing the shawl she held in her hands in the previous scene, and she is on her knees, rocking back and forth as if she is holding a baby. She is singing a lullaby.)

Mary: *(singing)* Sleep, little one, sleep. Sleep, little one, sleep. The eyes of God watch over you. Sleep, little one, sleep. *(She stops singing and looks at her hands. She realizes that they are empty. She pulls them up to her heart)* I used to sing that to him when he was a boy. It was a lullaby my mother would sing to me when I was frightened or hurt. It always comforted me to know she was close. *(pauses)* Jesus was always such a strong boy though, he wasn't afraid of anything. *(pauses)* But he did get hurt. The other children were not very ... kind to him. You know how children can be sometimes.

Jesus evoked such passionate responses in people. You could not ignore him, and those who loved him, loved him without reservation. But those who hated him, hated with an intensity that was frightening.

He would come home sometimes with scrapes and bruises and lay his head on my lap. I would stroke his hair and wash his cuts and I would sing to him. Sometimes he would cry, but most of the time he would just sigh. It was a deep, sorrowful, heart-breaking sigh and I would hear him whisper a prayer. It was always the same, forgive them Father, forgive them. And today I heard him pray that prayer again. Forgive them father ... *(cries)*

There is so much I don't understand. There is so much I have never understood. I was silent when the shepherds came on the day he was born to worship him. I was silent when the Magi came and offered him gifts and bowed down to him. I was silent when that old man prophesied over him at the temple, and I was silent when we found him in the temple talking with the Pharisees and scribes. I was silent because I was trying to understand. I was trying to understand God's plan.

It was obvious the hand of God was on him. It was on him like no one else in the history of our people. Everyone could see it, and they were amazed. I was amazed. I was amazed from the beginning, from the time the angel first appeared to me, but I could always see God's hand.

I could see his hand on him as he grew up into a wonderful man. He was so full of tenderness and joy. And his laughter! Oh, I loved to hear him laugh. I loved to watch him take little children on his knee and bless them just like a father would. I watched him heal the sick and raise the dead. I watched him feed thousands with just a little food. *(long pause with building emotion)* But I cannot see God's hand in *this*. I cannot see his plan. And I do not understand.

(angrily) I will never forget what happened to him. I will never forget what they did to my son. I will never forget the look on his face when he screamed to the heaven, "My God, my God, why have you forsaken me?" I will never forget the crown of thorns and the nails, the blood that he shed, and the tears that he cried. I will never forget what he prayed ... "Father, father, forgive them. They don't know what they're doing."

(long pause as she regains her composure) The sun is going down. But I cannot leave him. They are coming to take his body to somebody else's tomb.

(lights begin to fade) I cannot believe he's dead. My sweet boy, my son is dead. God's son ... is dead.

Blackout

Scene Three

(The lights come up on Sam who is now Alexander, a Roman soldier on crucifixion duty and he is not happy about it, either. He is standing center stage speaking to the audience who are a crowd at the crucifixion.)

Alexander: He's dead, people. Move along. I said he's dead, now move along. There won't be any more magic shows today. Let's go. Let's go. *(sarcastically)* It's just a little while before the Sabbath gets here so you better get home.

Come on, folks, what are you looking for? Another show? Looking for the sun to disappear and the earth to shake again? It's not going to happen, so move it! He's dead. Believe me. He's not going to be making any more trouble. Now get going or I'll be bringing some trouble your way, get me?

That's it. That's it. Keep it going. You'd think you people have never seen a crucifixion before the way you've been staring at this guy. He's nothing but a corpse, and you're standing there looking at him like he's going to come back from the dead or something. Believe me, he's not coming back. I made sure of that. I watched the blood come gushing out of him when I stuck him with this *(holds up spear)* and he didn't even move, so I know he won't be moving now.

Hey, pal. What are you staring at? I thought I told all of Jews to get out of here. What's that? What do I care what your name is? Oh, you were one of his followers, huh? Wait a minute, I remember you. You were the one down front with that woman, right? Who was that, his mother or something? That's what I thought. Why these mothers want to come to these things is something I'll never understand. Who wants to watch their son die like that? What'd you say your name was again? Oh, yeah, John. Okay, John, you get a good enough look? You ready to move along like a nice little Jew boy or do you need a little more persuasion?

(pauses as he listens to "John" and then looks uncomfortable) No, I didn't know who he was. Well, of course I had heard of him, but I never met the guy or anything. He was some kind of teacher or something right? Excuse me? Did you say Messiah? The Son of God? I'm no Jew, pal, what do I care if the guy thought he was the Messiah? In fact, why should I care even if he *was* the Messiah? If he's not one of my gods, then I'm not interested. Besides, none of my gods would have let themselves be nailed to a cross like this guy, I'll tell you that.

(pauses again) What do you mean you heard what I said when he died? What did I say? *(beat)* No, I didn't say that. No, I didn't. You have me confused with someone else. You know us Romans,

we all look alike to you people. *(angrily)* Look, pal, I said I didn't say it. Now shut up and get out of here! *(yelling after him)* I never said he was the Son of God, you hear me? I never said he was the Son of God!

Stupid Jew. *(pauses)* So what if I did say it? I was scared. After all, the guy died and sun disappears, for crying out loud. And he was a weird one to begin with. Most guys fight and kick and scream when we nail them down but this guy just lay there and let us do it. And he was staring at us the whole time with this weird look in his eyes, even while he was screaming from the pain he just stared at us with this look of ... pity. Yeah ... pity. And then when we got him up there he asked his father to forgive us. I've never heard that before, never. And I'll never forget that look.

(becoming angry again) Who was he to pity me, anyway? He was the one hanging on a cross with people laughing and spitting on him, not me! He was the one on the cross and I was the one who put him there! Who was he to ask anyone to forgive me? I don't need his forgiveness! He was the stinking criminal who got what he deserved, not me! *(brief pause)* He was no Son of God; I don't care what people say about him. I don't know who or what he was, but there is no way I would have killed the Son of God.

(turns to face the cross, which is offstage left) Who are you? I said, *Who are you?* Answer me if you're God! I heard about the miracles you performed and the things that you taught. You even healed my best friend's servant with just a word from your mouth. But if you could do all that, then why did you just let us put you on a cross? Why didn't you stop us? *(brief pause)* It's your own fault you're up there. You could have stopped it. I know you could have. You must have wanted to die. But who wants to die? Who wants to die like this?

How could you just let us kill you? How could you let us kill the Son of God?

Blackout

Scene Four

(It is dawn at the tomb of Jesus. Alexander is standing guard. He paces nervously center stage, his spear in hand. He thinks he hears a noise and jumps into a stance of attack.)

Alexander: Halt! Who goes there? *(realizes that it was nothing and gets angry at his own nervousness)* Come on, Alexander, you're acting like a green recruit. Shake it off. You've stood guard hundreds of times, this time is no different. *(pauses and looks offstage left)* Still, to stand guard over the tomb of the guy I just crucified days ago is more than a little creepy. The captain said that the powers that be were afraid his disciples would come and take the body, but something in his eyes told me we were out here for a different reason.

(looks out into the audience) Marcus! Stay awake over there! You know the penalty for sleeping on duty. Nobody falls asleep on my watch, got it? Don't make me warn you again ...

(The sounds of the tomb opening begin. Alexander reacts in confusion at first, with the confusion giving way to fear. He tries to steady himself and his men) Easy boys. Easy. Stand your ground, there's nothing to be afraid of ... I said, "Stand your ground!" *(looks at the tomb and terror crawls over his face)* You. You! It can't be. You're dead. I killed you! I saw you die! Please ... please I was just following orders. I had to do it ... I *(falls to his knees)* ... You can't be alive. You can't be. *(falls to his face)*

Blackout

Scene Five

(It is dawn. The lights come up on a hidden room where the disciples are nervously waiting, for what they do not know. Alexander has now become Peter.)

Peter: The sun is up. *(pauses)* So what are we going to do? Sit in here another day ... waiting? I don't know, you tell me, Andrew. What *are* we waiting for? Oh please, John, don't start that again. I

78

don't know about anybody else, but I'm sick of hearing that story. Yes, I know what he said, John, but he said a lot of things. He said the kingdom was near, but now we're all hiding out in some room like a bunch of rats while our king lies dead in a grave. Yeah, that's some kingdom.

(long pause) I'm sorry, John ... I ... I didn't mean to be so harsh. *(beat)* You know me. Old loud mouth Peter. I never know when to shut up. *(laughs nervously)* Yeah ... I never know when to shut up.

Like the time we saw him up on the mountain. Remember, John? Wow! What a sight. I just kept babbling on until God himself had to come down and tell me to be quiet. Or the time I kept arguing with everyone about who the greatest in the kingdom was going to be. I was so sure it was going to be me. Some joke, huh? And then there was the time, not too long ago, that I told him that even if everyone else deserted him, I never would. But there I was, running away. I was so scared I didn't even know what I was running to. And then, let us never forget the time that I said I would rather die than deny him. Even when he told me I would. Not once, but three times! No! Not me, Jesus! Not me! Even if everyone else denies you, I would rather die first! *(breaks down sobbing)*

I denied him, John. I denied him. I told them I didn't know him. I called down curses on myself and I swore I didn't know him! And did I cower away from some Roman soldier, a priest, or a Pharisee? Not me. Who was I afraid of? I was afraid of a girl, a little servant girl who was following me around the courtyard. *(cries again)*

(long pause) So you see, John, even if he did come back, he wouldn't want to see me. He wouldn't want to see any of us, John. Besides what can I do for my king if I can't even confess my allegiance in response to a little girl?

(Mary Magdalene enters. She has just seen Jesus and it shows.)

Mary Magdalene: Peter, John, everybody! It's him! It's him!

Peter: Who, Mary? Who are you talking about?

Mary Magdalene: *(trying to catch her breath)* I just saw ... I just saw ...

Peter: *(trying to calm her)* Who did you see, Mary?

Mary Magdalene: Jesus!

Peter: *(recoils)* What?

Mary Magdalene: I just saw Jesus!

Peter: Mary Magdalene, you're out of your head.

Mary Magdalene: No, Peter, I saw him.

Peter: Impossible.

Mary Magdalene: It's true.

Peter: You saw someone else that looked like him.

Mary Magdalene: No Peter, it was him. I know it. He spoke to me.

Peter: *(with venom)* You're lying.

Mary Magdalene: *(hurt)* Peter.

Peter: *(gentler now)* It wasn't him, Mary. You're upset. We all are. You wanted to see him, you believed what he said about coming back, and so your mind played a trick on you.

Mary Magdalene: *(firmly)* Peter, it was him.

Peter: No.

Mary Magdalene: Peter ...

Peter: No! *(pauses)* Speak no more of this Mary.

Mary Magdalene: I must tell you ...

Peter: I said to speak no more of this!

Mary Magdalene: Don't you bark orders at me, Simon Peter! I am not out of my head. I am not upset, and I *did* see him! He's alive! I saw him in the garden moments ago. So did his mother and John's mother, too. We were going to anoint his body with spices, and as we walked, we realized that there would be no one to roll the stone away from the tomb for us, but when we arrived we saw that the stone had already been rolled away!

And there, sitting on the stone were two of the most wonderful creatures I had ever seen. Their clothes were as bright as lightning and they spoke with powerful voices.

"Why do you look for the living among the dead?" they asked. "He is not here, he is risen, just as he said, come see the place where he lay." So we looked and he was gone Peter. He had come out of the tomb alive!

We left as quickly as we could to tell you and we met him on the road. He spoke to us, Peter. I saw him and I heard his voice. He is alive.

Peter: *(has been listening intently the whole time, as if in a trance)* Oh, Mary ... oh, Mary. What will I do now? I denied him, Mary, I denied him. I couldn't bear to look at him again.

Mary Magdalene: *(tenderly)* Oh, Peter. Don't you know that he'll forgive you?

Peter: How could he forgive me?

Mary Magdalene: We're talking about the Master, Peter. We're talking about Jesus.

Peter: No. For me there is no forgiveness.

Mary Magdalene: He asked for you, Peter.

Peter: What?

Mary Magdalene: He asked for you. He mentioned you by name.

Peter: He did?

Mary Magdalene: Yes.

Peter: *(begins crying for joy)* Oh, Mary. Do you think? Do you think he has, that he could?

Mary Magdalene: Of course, Peter. He loves you. You know he'll forgive you.

Peter: Jesus. Jesus! *(begins to exit stage left)*

Mary Magdalene: Peter, wait, where are you going?

Peter: I have to go see for myself. I have to know. *(exits stage left, yelling as he goes)* John. Come on. You were right. He's alive!

Blackout

Scene Six
(It is the Easter sunrise service. Karen and Sam are standing center stage with their arms raised high in praise. They lower their arms and smile at one another. The lighting and music should reflect an attitude of worship.)

Karen: The sun is up.

Sam: On Resurrection Sunday.

Karen: *(with feeling) Resurrection* Sunday. Can you feel it?

Sam: Yes. I can. *(laughs)* You know it's been so long, I had almost forgotten what real joy felt like.

Karen: *(laughs with him)* Me, too. This is wonderful.

Sam: *(pauses)* Look, everyone's leaving.

Karen: Does that mean it's over?

Sam: I hope not.

Karen: *(pauses)* We can't let it get old again, Sam.

Sam: It won't. Not if we live it.

Blackout